Transparent and intangible

as sunlight, yet always and

everywhere present, [the desert]

lures a man on and on, from

the red-walled canyons

to the smoke-blue

ranges beyond, in a

futile but fascinating

quest for the great,

unimaginable treasure which

the desert seems to promise.

Once caught by this golden lure

you become a prospector for life.

—EDWARD ABBEY
Desert Solitaire, 1968

Organ Pipe Cactus

NATIONAL MONUMENT

WHERE EDGES MEET

Bill Broyles

Principal Photography by George H. H. Huey

SOUTHWEST PARKS AND MONUMENTS ASSOCIATION
TUCSON, ARIZONA

Copyright ©1996 by Bill Broyles
All rights reserved

Published by Southwest Parks and Monuments Association
221 N. Court St.
Tucson, AZ 85701

Design and production by Amanda Summers

Illustrations by Barbara Terkanian, pages 12, 20, 23, 28, 32, 52, 56
Photometric map on page 37 by Jon Arnold and Tom Potter,
    Organ Pipe Cactus National Monument
Padre Kino's map of New Spain courtesy of Organ Pipe Cactus National Monument.

Additional photography: G.C. Kelly, pages 7, 14 (javelina and deer), 59, 60 (bobcat); Allen Morgan, pages 18 (ironwood blossom), 40 (ruddy duck), 41 (heron), 60 (oriole); Jack Dykinga, pages 18 (ironwood tree), 19 (globemallow), 42; Paul and Shirley Berquist, pages 21 (javelina), 21 (quail and coyote), 35; Frank Zullo, pages 34, 36; Rob Curtis, page 39; Jerry Jacka pages 43, 44 (projectile points); Peter L. Kresan, page 44 (petroglyph); Organ Pipe Cactus National Monument, pages 45 (ki), 46, 47, 48, 49, 50 (Cipriano house), 51 (Victoria Leon), 53; Arizona Historical Society, pages 45 (basket weavers), 50 (Francisco Villa and Jefferson Milton).

Quotation on page 1 reprinted by permission of Don Congdon Associates, Inc.

The net proceeds from SPMA publications support educational and research programs in your national parks.

 Printed on recycled paper.

Contents

This is organ pipe cactus country, land where edges meet. If you dance in your heart to the music of life, you'll love it. If you think it's pretty so far, you'll absolutely melt in its beauty later. If you are still looking for its charm, be patient. You are about to see the world anew.

Some visitors to Organ Pipe Cactus National Monument arrive fearing the worst. They expect a bleak nowhere punctuated by barren nothings. And why shouldn't they? After all, to get here they've driven past shifting sand dunes, salted fields, jagged basalt, and a dead mine heaped with rubble. They've overheard words like *malpais* (bad country) and *El Gran Desierto* (the biggest, baddest desert country).

Legend contends that on his initial visit the monument's first superintendent didn't even see the park and drove clear into Mexico before someone turned him around. He stayed for the best years of his life. Ominous? Empty? Hardly.

A first visit to the ocean may be dreary and gray. A first look at a glacial-fed river may be through voracious hoards of mosquitoes. A day trip to view a snow-capped summit may be obscured by scudding clouds. But eventually, inevitably, these rewarded us with indelible memories. And so it is with the desert. At first introduction it hides behind glare and protects itself with spines. It rebuffs our demand for instant understanding; it dares us to be patient.

Flowering brittlebush surrounds an organ pipe cactus

Appreciation comes in fits and surprises. We now see something where we saw nothing. A monotonous cross-country hike explodes in whir of Gambel's quail. A warm spring day throbs with the golden flashes of a million poppy petals. A dog-day of summer erupts with blazes of lightning silhouetting cactus spires. A scented breeze whistles through saguaro spines, singing fresh songs of self.

Who would expect to find shrimp in the desert? They're here. So are lichen, as far as the eye can see. Mosses, ferns, shore birds, snails, and mistletoe? You bet. And even stranger things: cactus fifty feet tall; mammals that never need to drink; fish that thrive where most would turn belly up; squirrels that hibernate in summer as well as winter; cactus with more arms than we have fingers and toes.

Organ Pipe Cactus National Monument draws nature lovers from around the globe. It spins at the geographical and biological center of the Sonoran Desert. Its purpose is to protect and explain, study and share this glorious land. Other deserts have great parks, but for deep desert, there's no place quite like Organ Pipe. In the kingdom of parks it ranks as many people's favorite.

One park ranger, approached by a wide-eyed but fidgety tourist, was asked, "What would you do here if you had only two hours to visit the monument?" The ranger blinked and replied somberly, "I'd cry."

Welcome. Bienvenidos. Ṣa: 'am 'a'i masma.

Cactus wren

With its tasty fruit, the organ pipe cactus symbolizes the desert's bounty and is a delectable favorite of desert dwellers. A many-stemmed cactus without any apparent trunk, it resembles an old-fashioned pipe organ playing in this Sonoran sanctuary. Some eminent specimens grow twenty-five feet tall and have a hundred arms. Each arm, pleated with twelve to nineteen ridges, looks almost friendly enough to hug.

In May or June the organ pipe cactus flowers open as the sun slides behind the ridge. The livid bud slowly, imperceptibly, pushes open its clenched tips, revealing an unforgettable blossom. In a realm of greens and browns, it is a swatch of splendor, a cream-colored banner in the night hoisted on tall, spiny arms. Its scent is faint, but a moth could no more miss its three-inch face than we can overlook a full moon. Nighttime moths and bats spread pollen from one flower to another, and an assortment of daytime ants, bees, flies, and even birds may visit the fading beauty. Each arm may produce dozens of flowers, but no more than one or two bloom on any given night, a strategy that encourages cross-pollination with distant plants and reduces in-breeding.

The fruit grows to the size of a plum. Spines guard its ripening, but drop away when it reddens, and the feast begins. The fruit may split on its own, but eager Gila woodpeckers

Spreading stems of the organ pipe cactus

stand ready to peck it open. Birds gorge themselves on its pulp and seeds, bees wallow in its sweet juice, and ground squirrels brave a ladder of spines for even a taste. The fruit is a staple of the lesser long-nosed bat (*Leptonycteris curasoae*). Any fruit that falls to the ground is quickly discovered and devoured by grateful coyotes and javelinas. None is wasted.

People, too, relied on the fruit for sustenance. The Tohono O'odham still harvest this tasty treat along with fruit of the saguaro. Early summer was and is a time of feasting and thanksgiving. Some fruit was eaten fresh from the cactus, for who could resist its flavor like sugared watermelon. The rest was made into drink or dried for storage, and its seeds pounded into flour.

A single fruit contains nearly two thousand seeds and a large plant may produce fifty fruits per year, but it takes hundreds of fruits to generate even one heir. Although most seeds are fertile—up to 92 percent of them—they must evade a gauntlet of mouths, sun, and catastrophe. The few seedlings that survive their first fifteen years have a solid chance for a full life. In the wild an organ pipe cactus takes eight perilous years to reach a height of four inches. By its nineteenth birthday it may be three feet tall, and it may attain its full height of twenty feet by age forty-five.

A cactus with multiple arms has several advantages over single-stemmed plants. More arms allow them to store additional water while

Cactus Music

Dawn catches the night-blooming cereus

Senita cactus

Organ pipe and saguaro cactus

at the same time increasing their surface area of chlorophyll for photosynthesis, enabling adults to grow more vigorously. Also, more arms permit production of more flowers and seeds, increasing the odds that the species will survive. And, the more arms a plant has, the less affected it is by injury to any one limb.

Organ pipe cacti flourish in Sonora and Sinaloa, Mexico, but this monument presents the finest gathering in the United States. A few renegades grow as far away as Tucson and Phoenix, but frost, not heat, restrains forests of them from growing further northward.

Scientifically named *Stenocereus thurberi*, the organ pipe cactus is related to other tall, candle-shaped cacti in the cereus group. *Steno* refers to its narrowness, and *thurberi* honors George Thurber, the first person to scientifically describe it. He was one of the most accomplished horticulturists in America and accompanied William Emory's 1850-1854 survey of the United States/Mexico boundary. Other cereus include the saguaro, senita, cardon, and night-blooming cereus. In Mexico thousands of acres of these magnificent cacti are bull-dozed annually to clear land for cattle grazing, highlighting the need for their protection within Organ Pipe Cactus National Monument.

At first glance the senita cactus resembles the organ pipe in size and shape; both have no main trunk and many vertical stems. However, the senita's distinctive gray spines resemble a scraggly beard on the tips of the stems, inspiring common names like "old man" cactus. It also has fewer ribs in each arm, only six or seven, and these are more deeply fluted. Like the organ pipe its pale pink flowers are nocturnal and its fruit eaten by animals and people alike, though flower and fruit are only half the size of the organ pipe cactus's. Mature plants annually produce an average of 125 fruits, each holding 200 seeds.

More than half of new senita plants are established asexually, without seeds, when stems fall to the ground and take root. Some fallen stems are caught in flashfloods and carried to new homes. Because they are succulent—their pulp retains water through drought, they may survive many months until rooting. Senitas grow better in deeper, sandier soils of valleys and plains, but organ pipe cacti thrive on sun-drenched hillsides, where they can anchor their roots in the rocky ground.

Senitas are even more frost sensitive than organ pipes. Virtually all of the few hundred native senitas in the United States grow only in the monument, in a sheltered, granite cove named for them—Senita Basin. They are common in the Mexican state of Sonora.

Armed with forbidding spines and storing their own canteen of water, senitas and organ pipes appear ready for anything, but they are slightly delicate and very fickle. Not just any hot or dry spot will do. They do not grow in other American deserts.

The Sonoran Desert is the most lush and most diverse desert in all the world. Its mild winters and two rainy seasons encourage these plants to prosper by providing *two* extended growing seasons. The Mojave, Chihuahuan, or Great Basin deserts have but one. Although the monument averages seventeen freezing nights a year, these cold spells last only for a few hours each.

Even here in a desert, cacti are limited by cold. Their succulent stems, which store water to sustain them through summer's heat, work against them when temperatures fall below freezing for more than a few hours. The water inside individual cells freezes, fatally bursting the cell wall or, worse, an entire stem freezes

Organ pipe fruit

LEFT: *Organ pipe flower*

and splits, exposing it to disease. Stems and arms are lost, growth tips are ruined, and the main trunk may die.

In what sounds like a contradiction, the Sonoran Desert was born in the tropics. Our large column-like cacti and trees, including the mesquites, paloverdes, and ironwood, evolved from tropical and nearly tropical relatives. When glaciers of the last ice age receded toward the pole and temperatures in Mexico and Arizona warmed, tropical plants spread northward. Organ pipe cacti

Why Are Cacti Prickly?

Cacti are canisters of sugar-water in a thirsty land, but they're not entirely defenseless. Their leaves evolved into spines. The longer ones, ranging from the sizes of needles up to nails, are called central and radial spines, but anyone who bumps into a cactus may longer remember the smaller, barbed bristles called glochids, which ratchet into the skin like tiny splinters. Obviously, spines deter animals from devouring such a succulent morsel, but in the driest of times even spines can't fend off rabbits and mice (which nibble between the rows of spines), javelina and cattle (which eat spines and all), or bighorn sheep (which butt barrel cacti to split them open and eat the succulent pulp).

Fortunately for cacti, spines are not their only defense. Cacti have waxy skins that resist small mouths and their pulp is acidic, a key to fending off infections. Their pasty inner fluids suffocate and stymie insect larvae. And, cacti produce a number of unfriendly alkaloid chemicals that taste bitter, are toxic, or inhibit infections.

Spines also have other jobs. Jumping and teddy bear cholla are notorious for greeting us with a firm grip, but their joints are just hitch-hiking to any new neighborhood. Many cactus fruits have spines that catch in the fur of animals to help spread the seeds.

Spines clothe the cactus, creating a microhabitat. They help shade the apical growth-tip on cactus stems from too much sun and heat. In some cacti this "straw hat" furnishes 30 to 80 percent shade. In winter, spines help hold in warmth and, though rarely needed, provide insulation against snow. Study of the spine density and pattern on the apical tip can predict the species' northern limits by telling how warmly it's dressed. Spines also funnel rain or even dew toward the roots of the cactus, and may reduce the drying or chilling effects of wind, as well as acting as "bumpers" against injury from careless feet or the rubbing limbs of its nurse tree.

appear in the monument's fossil record about thirty-five hundred years ago, and the saguaro eleven thousand years ago. Cacti themselves evolved about fifty million years ago in a dry region of northern South America, possibly descending from a now extinct member of the cactus-like genus *Pereskia*.

Although species of cactus grow in many states and provinces of North America, most cacti require plentiful sunlight and hot days. They also must have occasional rains and cooler evenings to carry them through the heat. They don't grow in the hottest or driest or saltiest of desert places, even in the Sonoran Desert. Too little or too infrequent rainfall and they can't ration their stored water. With too much rainfall, they struggle against faster growing plants, and they drown when their roots can't breathe, falling victim to root rot. Cacti grow best in places receiving between six and fifteen inches of rain per year. In parts of the monument, such as the Valley of the Ajo and western Growler Valley, the soil may be too dry for big

Chain fruit cholla flower in rain

cactus, but no parts are too hot—columnar cactus do fine until the air temperature repeatedly hits 131 degrees Fahrenheit, which is higher than any ever recorded here.

Plants use light to make energy. They take in carbon dioxide, sunlight, and water to produce sugars and starches. In this chemical process, excess oxygen is produced and must be exhaled through the plant's pores (stomata). Most types of plants breathe during the day, when light is strongest. But if desert plants open their pores to breathe during the hottest part of the day, they lose valuable moisture.

So, to cope with heat and drought, cacti have developed several strategies. Long ago they abandoned leaves (which transpire water), added wide-reaching roots to catch even slight rains, and pumped themselves with water-storing pulp. Moreover, they evolved a whole new metabolism called CAM—short for Crassulacean Acid Metabolism. In effect, cacti hold their breaths all day and resume breathing at night, when the oxygen wastes are released

Barrel cactus and teddy bear cholla

Flowering barrel cactus

Saguaro cactus in bloom

Engelmann's hedgehog cactus

13

*Great horned owl nestlings
in saguaro cactus nest*

and carbon dioxide is absorbed for photosynthesis the next day. A graph of CAM activity shows a sudden and steep rise at sundown and an equally precipitous drop at sunup. During the day exchanges of carbon dioxide and water vapor hover at zero. This special photosynthesis minimizes water loss on torrid days.

But CAM does have drawbacks. Growth is slow and irregular, so seldom is cactus the dominant plant. And cacti cannot survive excessively hot temperatures because they cannot transpire and cool themselves by evaporation during the day. Finally, since they can pull water only out of wet soil, cacti "drink" for just short periods after rains.

The conditions that permit adult cacti to prosper are not the same that encourage the young to grow. A string of exceptionally wet summers is necessary to germinate the seed and sustain the seedlings, which

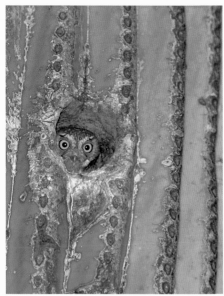

Javelina eating prickly pear

Mule deer eating cholla

RIGHT: *Elf owl in saguaro cactus nest*

start life as dicotyledons—two tasty leaves on a stem. Gambel's quail eat them; thrashers dig them up; rabbits and rodents think they're candy. Of the millions of seeds cast by one parent, maybe one plant will grow to adulthood.

Cactus seeds have a short viability period. Those of organ pipes, for example, are designed to scatter in June, feel rain in July, and sprout in August. Those lying on the ground after that are unlikely to ever germinate, having lost their viability or been eaten by rodents and birds. Cacti raised from seed in greenhouses have far better odds for survival, and specimens of most Sonoran Desert plants can be found for sale in specialty plant nurseries throughout the Southwest.

The lucky cactus seed sprouts under the guardianship of a nurse-plant, a tree or shrub that covers and conceals it. One study found virtually all saguaro seedlings in sheltered places, with 89 percent of them under bursages or paloverdes. Even 71 percent of the more heat-tolerant barrel cacti were found under protective plants, with half of them in clumps of grass.

Here is a paradox, though. Seedlings and young cacti nestled within nurse shrubs receive less sunlight and must compete with the shrub itself for water, so they grow slower than if they were in the open. But, these problems are offset by what is gained—nitrogen enriched soil, predator protection, and moderation of temperature extremes.

Probably more photos are taken of the twenty-eight species of cacti growing in the monument than any other subject. After all, cactus is the monument's middle name.

Ages

Typical life spans:

fairy shrimp 2-3 weeks

Mexican gold poppy 2-4 months

cigarette butt 1-5 years

red-tailed hawk 6-10 years

tarantula 10 years

bighorn sheep 10-12 years

bullsnake 15-22 years

desert tortoise 30-80 years

bursage 50-100 years

humans 70-100 years

ant colony > 100 years

paloverde 100-150 years

saguaro 150-200 years

ironwood 1000-1500 years

creosote 1,000-10,000 years

glass bottle 1,000,000 years

Considering this is a desert, few first-time visitors expect plants and animals to be such a grand part of the Organ Pipe Cactus National Monument story. But they are. At last count 589 plant species and subspecies grow within the monument boundaries, representing almost one-third the total for the entire Sonoran Desert. Birds? Two hundred seventy-seven species have been seen here, along with seventy species of mammals (including fourteen bats), five native species of toads, two turtles, fifteen lizards, and twenty-four snakes. Imagine seventy-seven known species of butterflies! Not bad for a desert.

Biologically the Sonoran Desert is the richest and most diverse of North America's four arid regions. It covers nearly 120,000 square miles, with 516 square miles of it found within Organ Pipe Cactus National Monument. Because of its crossroads location, the monument has an exceptionally wide range of special plants and animals. Here is a unique medley of terrain, water, climate, soil, and living things. Here the ranges of a host of species overlap one another, providing a rich blend of food and habitat that makes this desert community what it is. The study of these relationships is ecology.

Some species—columnar cactus, nectar-feeding bats, boas, Gila monsters—accompanied the Sonoran Desert as it moved north from the

A mix of cactus and trees in the Arizona Upland plant community

sub-tropics. Others, the smoke tree and desert tortoise, stayed behind when the Sonoran drifted into what had been the Mojave Desert. Woodland plants and animals, from cooler and wetter mountains, remained when the glaciers retreated, resulting in populations of oak, juniper, and white-tailed deer in the highest reaches of this desert park.

Other plants and animals adapted from species already living around the Gulf of California. These include the elephant tree, limberbush, salt grass, and the sidewinder. Some plants—bursages and saltbushes, for example—are descendants of readily adaptable species already living here.

Organ Pipe Cactus National Monument straddles two Sonoran Desert plant communities, the Lower Colorado River Valley and the Arizona Upland, and it includes elements of a third, the Central Gulf Coast. Representing the hottest of the Sonoran Desert zones, the Lower Colorado River Valley community is composed primarily of three groups: saltbush; creosote and bursage; and a mix of brittlebush, creosote, and bursage.

The Arizona Upland community consists of our two most luxuriant groups. The mix cactus and foothill palove group covers about one-ha of this monument and includes most of the large cacti, many ironwood and mesquite trees, and spring wildflowers galore. The other group—jojoba and evergreen scrubland—is found in slightly wetter and higher terrain and consists of jojoba, agave, rose-

Neighbors in Concert

Western banded gecko

Individual ironwood flowers

Ironwood tree in full bloom

Elephant tree, a representative of the Central Gulf Coast community

wood, and juniper. The trail to Bull Pasture rises through this subdivision.

A flavor of the Central Gulf Coast community is represented in Organ Pipe by the elephant tree, senita, and limberbush. These can be seen on the drive to Senita Basin.

Trees, another tropical gift to this desert, spread northward when the climate warmed. These include the blue paloverde, foothill paloverde, ironwood, mesquite, and acacia. Most of their relatives live in tropical and subtropical zones, but here they developed new traits, such as dropping their leaves in drought and spreading their roots farther and deeper. The other American deserts have some trees, but trees in the Sonoran Desert are larger and play far more prominent roles.

No tree is more symbolic of the heart of the Sonoran Desert than the ironwood. With its tropical heritage, it loves heat and hates frost. Its protective limbs spread over an incredible nursery of young plants. In one study, sixty-five plant species were associated with ironwood and only eight preferred growing away from it. The advantage isn't just shade. Fallen leaves enrich the soil and provide a mulch cover to retain moisture. The roots of the ironwood, as with most legumes, add essential nitrogen to the soil. Here seedlings are hidden from sun, drought, and toothy critters.

Other plants, too, serve as nurses. Besides ironwood, the best are dense, bushy perennials such as bursage, brittlebush, goldeneye, and paloverde, each of which provides up to 50 percent shade as well as the other amenities. Creosote gives less than 20 percent shade, so it is not favorable for young cacti and trees, but its rodent-stirred soil and leaf litter make fine niches for winter and spring annuals that bloom before the searing onset of summer. Few seedlings of any species find refuge under the columnar cacti.

Soil is a crucial and complex part of the ecology. When wind rakes the desert, we might expect billowing Sahara-like dust storms, but they seldom happen here because the soil is blanketed by a matted crust of lichen and algae. This crust functions as the desert's skin, protecting it and holding in moisture. Called cryptobiotic (hidden life) soil, it's a complicated partnership of cyanobacteria, green algae, mosses, lichens, bacteria, fungi, and tiny animals in a symbiotic relationship. The cyanobacteria, algae, lichen, and mosses convert sunlight to energy. Then the fungi, bacteria, and animals feed off them and return the favor by providing moisture and nutrients.

Cryptobiotic soil is usually seen as black or green crusts on the ground, especially in sandy flats. It binds the topsoil together with living strands and it carpets more ground than all other plants combined. The cryptobiotic team is exceptionally hardy in drought and heat. It may go years without rain or dew, but will resume growing within minutes after receiving water. However, because of its slow growing pace, it takes decades to develop. Disturbance by cattle, off-road driving, and digging are injuries that heal very slowly. Desert plants rely on this cryptobiotic crust to retain moisture

in the soil and to prevent nutrients from blowing or washing away.

Desert soils are low in humus —one-tenth of that found in humid regions. Humus provides the food necessary for plants to grow. Next to water, nitrogen is the most needed

Organ pipe cactus and teddy bear cholla

and least available ingredient in this soil. Phosphorus, calcium, iron, and trace minerals are abundant, as are the soil microorganisms such as bacteria, streptomycetes, fungi, yeasts, protozoa, and algae necessary to translate chemistry into plant growth.

Mountain slopes, too, have soil covers. In addition to cryptobiotic soils, spike mosses and ferns form thick mats, helping hold and fertilize the soil. These are prominent in the Ajo Mountains along the Bull Pasture trail and on most north-facing slopes.

With a soil poor in humus and

Globemallow and purple phacelia

Ant Farmers

We've all heard of ant farms, but Mexican leaf-cutting ants (*Atta mexicana*) are true farmers. Their colonies, remnants of the Sonoran Desert's tropical heritage, actually farm fungus. Fewer than forty colonies, all in the monument, are known in the United States.

Colonies prefer nesting on the banks of large arroyo channels and may extend six feet below the surface, with hundreds of side tunnels and chambers. Exits may be as far as 120 yards from the central opening. Using up to thirty trails simultaneously, a colony can forage over two to five acres.

By day in winter and by night in summer, workers leave the nest to forage. They climb plants and cut leaves, dropping them to the ground for other ants to pick up and carry home. They seldom take so many leaves to kill the plant, and their nests actually help plants by mixing air and humus into the soil and by letting rainwater drain deeply into the ground. A colony may collect up to four hundred pounds of vegetation per year. The ants use 75 percent of the types of available shrubs and trees, but they prefer creosote leaves and flowers in fall and winter, and then paloverde flowers and leaves in the spring. The ants avoid bursages and brittlebush.

But for all their work, these ants don't actually eat the leaves or flowers. Down in the nest, chambers of leaves are mulched and then "seeded" with fungus. Not just any fungus, mind you, but a venerable one traditional with this colony. It is like a starter yeast handed down from generation to generation; queens leaving the nest take a dollop with them for the next colony. In the tropics, from where these ants came, clonal lines of ant-farmed fungus approach 23 million years of history. The ants keep their fungus rooms near 100 percent humidity at 80 degrees Fahrenheit. The fungus grows, giving the ants their own supermarket and complete diet. Some ants are even employed to weed this garden, lest another fungus ruin the crop.

This is an example of symbiosis, a process by which two species help each other. The ants need the fungus for food, but the fungus also needs the ants. The fungus has domesticated the ants as much as the ants have domesticated it.

low in nitrogen, decaying plants are all the more important to those still living and generations to come. Saguaro and cholla skeletons, once prized by hobbyists who made lamps and furniture of them, decay slowly. They, as well as dead paloverdes and other woody plants, are attacked by woodpeckers, termites, and beetles that break down the wood into smaller pieces and then into powdery fertilizer. They also provide niches in which seeds may grow, and homes for important insects,

lizards, and small mammals. Ants, termites, and rodents are especially important in stirring the soil and in moving humus to their dens. These are the desert's soil makers, allowing air and water to circulate. Soil compacted even 20 percent loses its fertility; dirt roads last driven fifty years ago—the old Ajo-Sonoyta trail, for instance—remain visible as hardened ruts.

Although vertebrate animals make up only one percent of living matter in the desert, they attract much of our interest. Fortunately, we needn't go far to see them. Any wash or canyon is a good place to start, as is the campground. In a wash we find Gambel's quail tracks and hear them clucking in the thick wolfberry. Mule deer tracks lead to a midday bed under a blue paloverde. We notice where javelina have torn into a prickly pear, eating pads and tearing up roots. Occasional coyote paths cut up the bank. A desert cottontail hops coyly into its thorny warren. Overhead, brown-crested flycatchers and phainopeplas flutter after insects, and ahead of us a curve-billed thrasher looking for insects sweeps the ground with its beak. Then we're startled by a squadron of frightened doves fleeing a hungry Cooper's hawk.

If we return by the creosote flat beyond the wash, we can expect to

spot a black-tailed jackrabbit crouched under a creosote, frozen so we won't see it. At any instant it may sprint away in a perplexing medley of loops and angles meant to confound even the wiliest coyote. A roadrunner plunges headlong through a cholla patch chasing after a zebra-tailed lizard. Overhead a red-tailed hawk wheels in the wind, its ever keen eyes searching below for any careless morsel. If we tire of walking, we can sit quietly on a rock or under a tree and let the animals come to us.

Sunset, too, is a good time for watching wildlife. Noisy quail vie for choice perches on mesquite limbs. In the twilight we hear an agitated verdin causing commotion in a creosote; neatly coiled at the base is a tiger rattlesnake waiting for a passing deer mouse. We hear a

thrasher's one-note warning twits and look for the great horned owl perched atop a saguaro. We would have to travel far southward to hear more than the six species of owls we do in Organ Pipe.

By looking away from the nighttime grill or lantern, we may find banded geckos, pocket mice with their cheeks stuffed, and male tarantulas out courting females. Coyotes howl distant messages to others in the pack. Plants learned by day become our gallery of silhou-etted friends at night.

Animals are tied to the cycles of leaves and seeds. Births of plant-eating animals are timed to coincide with growth of the plants on which they feed. Bighorn sheep, prong-horn, and deer are born in early spring, when nursing mothers can take advantage of reliable and

OPPOSITE PAGE: *Regal horned lizard*

LEFT TO RIGHT: *Tarantula, Gambel's quail, Coyote*

TOP OF PAGE: *Javelina*

Black-tailed jackrabbit

Merrium's Kangaroo rat

<small>RIGHT:</small> *Desert iguana*
Fledgling red-tailed hawk

succulent browse. Their young are mobile within a few hours after being born. Deer and pronghorn fawns are "hiders," lying in tall grass, unlike bighorn lambs, which follow their mothers everywhere, even across open rock faces. Gambel's quail chicks and jackrabbit babies also are precocious, born ready to go, but other newborns are helpless at birth and must be fed. Young cottontails and doves are blind and bald, requiring weeks before they can leave the nest or feed themselves.

Even the predators time their lives to plants, though indirectly. Carnivorous mountain lions are linked in the food chain to herbivorous deer, bobcats and coyotes and foxes to rodents and rabbits, horned lizards to ants, and robber flies to insects which suck on plant juices.

Several families of mountain lions live in and near the park, but they're secretive and seen only by lucky observers. The monument's estimated 120 bighorn sheep may be seen on steep slopes and ridges with binoculars, but in some seasons they browse ironwood trees in the arroyo bottoms. Deer bed by day and browse before dawn and after dusk. Javelina—noisy, contentious creatures with very poor eyesight— usually are heard before they're seen on the bajadas or near arroyo banks.

This unique mix of plants and animals provides a special charm and an unrivaled collection. If we used a cookie-cutter to carve out five hundred square miles of the very best Sonoran Desert plants, animals, and geology, we couldn't do better than Organ Pipe Cactus National Monument.

Bench Mark

A gentle hand slips the squalling pocket mouse from a cloth bag. The mouse is unhappy. Last night it followed a trail of oats into a strange hole that snapped shut behind it. Now it is being examined and charted: species, gender, weight. Finished, the hand sets the mouse on the ground, and the mouse scurries straight home, unharmed but with unbelievable stories to tell.

The same pocket mouse may be caught again tomorrow night, or the trap may entice a kangaroo rat or a grasshopper mouse. The trap is one of forty-nine laid out in a grid ninety meters on a side.

The theory is that in two nights of yearly trapping researchers will net 72 percent of all rodents in the zone. Their weights will be added, and the weights of all rodents in the monument calculated. Knowing this biomass, researchers can plot the land's productivity in the current year. Rodents are good indicators of the health of the land. A key link in the food chain: they eat seeds and leaves, and they in turn are consumed by hawks, snakes, foxes, and coyotes.

With habitat changing on a global scale, it is increasingly important to have yardsticks like Organ Pipe to measure changes. There are fewer undisturbed places to assess the extent and effects of pollution, desertification, ground water depletion, global warming, and invasive plants.

Some Old World plants, introduced to help us, have escaped into the hinterlands. Tamarisk, a Mediterranean native tree, does even better here than it did at home, and now it evicts willow, mesquite, and cottonwood along waterways and ponds. Fewer native animals and birds use the tamarisk, and it secretes salt which poisons the ground around it. In many places it chokes the rivers themselves, transpiring too much water and clogging the flow. If not for human intervention it would take over Quitobaquito as it has the Sonoyta River.

Similarly, buffelgrass from the savannah of Africa looks innocent enough. Sown on ranchlands for cattle feed, it crowds out other plants, strangling their roots and growing so thickly and pervasively that it creates square miles of tinder. When buffel burns, it kills trees, cacti, roots, and even the seeds of tomorrow. Red brome and fountain grass pose the same threats.

On a worldwide scale, arid lands research here is some of the finest. And as with any inquiry, one answer leads to a dozen questions. By learning what we have, where it's found, and how it lives, we can make informed decisions and save a special world for our tomorrow.

We lounge on smooth rock next to a pool of water high on the mountain. A dragonfly alights on the surface and daubs its tail to deposit eggs. Beneath the surface a water beetle stalks a tadpole. The immense Coahuila juniper tree shading us looks somehow out of place. So does the pool —a desert gem called a *tinaja*. Etched and pounded into bedrock by running water, tinajas catch canyon runoff, perhaps filling several times a year.

Sheer cliffs rise vertically on two sides, forming a flume. We're unsettled to see driftwood overhead and realize that occasionally a six-foot-deep train of water pounds through this slot in the Ajo Mountains, cutting the canyon ever deeper. A flashflood would spit us out of the notch like a watermelon seed. On a rainy day clouds would swirl around the tops of the Ajos and roll down the valley. The patter of raindrops would be followed by surging runnels and then short-lived falls would spill 50, 150, 300 feet. For a few hours Boulder Canyon would become a torrent and the walls of Estes Canyon spout two dozen sterling falls at once.

We worked hard to get here today, toting our packs up a switchback trail. We climbed a ladder of time, passing through epochs of rock and plants, as if seeking a lost plateau. On another day we will continue up the ridge and clamber for the summit, but

Tinaja in Ajo Mountains

today we're content to lie under this juniper in heaven. On the slopes grow oak and rosewood, which we would expect farther north on taller ranges. We're puzzled. But a rat has left the answer in its den.

Woodrats, also called pack rats (*Neotoma albigula*), are great collectors. Their dens are troves of food and trinkets. They pick up seeds and berries, tin foil and sticks, bones and bottle caps to make what amounts to an inverted "bird" nest on the ground or in a crevice. They eat what they can and cache the rest. Near each den is a pile for waste and junk. Urine cements this messy midden together in a very durable time capsule.

Researchers with microscopes and Geiger counters have read the debris in these middens back fourteen thousand years, giving us a glimpse of what was. The ancestors of this juniper overhead lived here when this place was a cool-climate woodland. The oak and rosewood were here then, too. Not until eleven millennia ago did mesquite, brittlebush, and saguaro appear in the local fossil record. Organ pipe, barrel, and cholla cacti arrived about thirty-five hundred years back.

About eleven thousand years ago the continental ice cap receded and global storm tracks shifted northward, giving this area warmer year-round temperatures and less winter rainfall. As the climate warmed and dried, juniper, oak, and rosewood disappeared except for these relics in the deeply shaded canyon bottoms and on sheltered,

High Country Rock

Wood rat

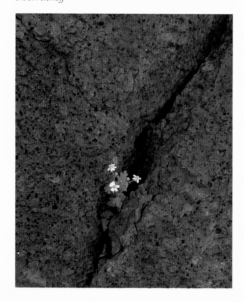

Rock daisy

*Summer thunderstorm,
Ajo Mountains*

*Western diamondback
rattlesnake*

north-facing slopes. Even today the Ajo range is wetter than the mountains to the west, averaging thirteen and one-half inches a year, while the Bates Mountains, sixteen hundred feet lower, average seven and one-half.

A desert is a dry place, where rapid evaporation exceeds precipitation. Flowing water is rare and perennial water lies hidden underground or trapped in tinajas like this one. Regions in the tropics may actually have higher yearly average temperatures than Organ Pipe, but their deluges of rainfall overwhelm any evaporation. Evaporation in Organ Pipe may exceed ten feet of standing water a year.

The Sonoran Desert is the Goldilocks of deserts: not too hot, not too cold, not too wet, not too dry; it is just right. Rainfall at the visitor center averages nine and three-quarters inches per year, with roughly half of that coming in summer and half in winter. It's this balance that places the Sonoran midway between its neighboring deserts. In the Mojave Desert rain comes primarily in winter; in the Chihuahuan Desert, primarily in summer. The desert to the north, the Great Basin, is cold as well as dry. The Sonoran's milder winters with fewer bouts of freezing permit a wider variety of plants to grow.

Shadows fill the canyon as we shoulder our packs for the descent to the valley. The afternoon sun slants low on the Ajo Mountains, and they glow warm and close. The volcanic rock reddens as if molten once again. Seen in dawn's glow of our early morning ascent, the backlit range loomed formidable and distant but now it appears personable and soft. To the west the Bates and the Puerto Blanco ranges now look sheer and foreboding, unscalable blank walls of dark mystery. These are remnants of larger mountains, mountains born of cataclysm and sundering stress. These are Basin and Range faulted volcanics, rugged, steep, and deeply torn.

To understand the geology of Organ Pipe we need to look one hundred miles west of here, where our North American plate bumps into the Pacific plate along the San Andreas Fault. Edges like this are exciting places to ride the continent, for when such massive plates collide, two violent things may happen. One plate may slide under part of the other, producing volcanoes. Or, one plate may snag the other and rip chunks of it away, causing extensive faults and earthquakes.

Both of these mighty forces have shaped Organ Pipe. Imagine this region as your dinner table with the places set and the food served. You slip your arm under the table cloth and slowly slide it across the table from west to east. The jumbled mess of dishes represents faulted and fractured mountains, and the spilled food becomes lava flows. As if this weren't enough, guests are slowly tugging on both ends of the table cloth, stretching it until it tears and then pulling it even farther. And during their continental tug-of-war, for good measure, you slowly slide your arm back across the entire table, which now suggests the grand chaos of Organ Pipe's mountains today.

The first process, your sliding arm, occurs when one plate slides under another. The lower plate is swallowed back into the earth's molten mantle, but as that rock is heated and melted into magma, it rises and tries to escape through the surface. If successful, it explodes and flows from volcanoes. If it does not push through the surface, it forms an enormous bulge of granite, which cools and is later exposed when the rock above it erodes.

The second process, pulling the table cloth, is faulting, and rocks— even mountains—are pulled apart.

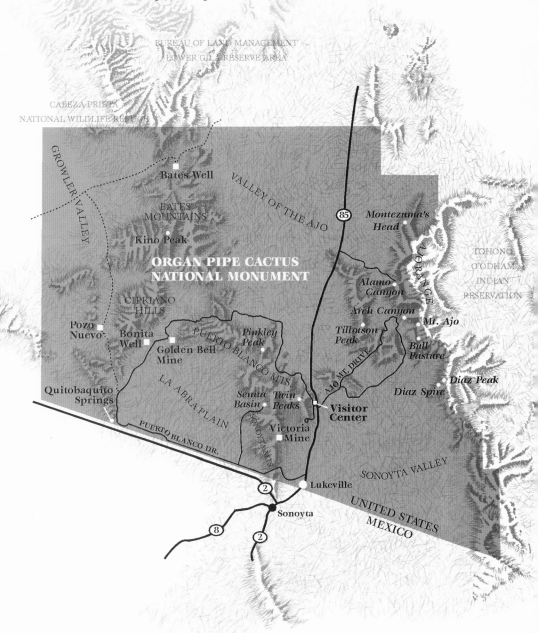

Who Makes the Holes?

Our step accidentally collapses the roof of a hidden tunnel, puffing dust out a distant entrance. We lift our foot and are startled by a squeak. Out hops a baby kangaroo rat, uninjured but greatly confused. Unseeing, unweaned, and vulnerable it stands in the glaring sun and cries like a squeeze-toy. We nudge it back to the cave-in and guiltily wonder what to do. It sits bawling, all mouth and whiskers and feet. A spoonful of sand slips deeper into the hole, then another. The tunnel yawns open as the youngster's mother snatches it by the nape and lunges back into the darkness, reuniting her brood and hurriedly packing the breach with sand.

For a place with such hard ground, Organ Pipe sure seems to have a lot of holes, but they are crucial for animals to survive heat and escape predators. The main diggers are rodents. With their large feet and claws, they tunnel easily and extensively, making dens for storing seeds and for raising young. As any hiker in the monument can attest, these pitfalls and underground freeways seem to lurk everywhere. The monument has seventeen kinds of rodents (mice, rats, and squirrels), each and all of them prodigious diggers. Many desert rodents are dormant during part of the summer as well as the winter.

Snakes can dig in soft soil or sand, but they usually usurp a burrow...after eating the owner. The shovel-nosed snake is aptly named, for it pushes its way through soft dirt in search of insects. Lizards dig shallow burrows with oval openings. Gila monsters and tortoises stay underground more than 95 percent of their lives. Tarantulas may not look like diggers, but they do excavate their own burrows and then make doors from webbing and pebbles to seal out rain and intruders.

Larger holes are usually the work of badgers, furry backhoes with claws one and one-half inches long. They carve out burrows for nesting, for afternoon shade, and for plundering rodent holes. Occasionally, large holes are excavated by denning coyotes.

The burrows of these animals help channel life-giving air and water to plant roots, whereas off-road driving and livestock grazing compact the soil, blocking air and water while increasing erosion from runoff.

This tension has stretched our region into what we see today as the unique Basin and Range Province, the only one of its kind on Earth. Here mountains rose and valleys fell when the land was stretched and torn. Think of a layer cake stacked on that table cloth; when the fabric was pulled taut, the cake broke apart, with some pieces standing tall and others slumping down. In geology, the taller pieces are called horsts, the mountains we see today, while the fallen slices are grabens, the bedrock of our wide, sediment-filled valleys.

Organ Pipe geology is relatively young. What we see here began less than 110 million years ago when the North American plate we're on rode westward over a smaller plate, the Farallon, pinching it against the Pacific plate. This produced a wave of volcanic mountain building from the Pacific coast eastward clear to central New Mexico. It was a slowly moving episode, called the Laramide Orogeny, occurring from 70 to 55 million years ago. It left a legacy of mountain building, now exposed by erosion, that forms our granite ranges of the Southwest. This wave left us the gentlest but oldest mountains in the monument. They are the little granitic "hills" of the Quitobaquito Hills and the Sonoyta Mountains, which 58 to 60 million years ago bulged under the surface and have since been eroded down to meek memories of their former stalwart selves.

And, throughout the region the

Laramide period of mountain building left extensive volcanic fields much like the Cascade volcanic region of the Northwest. These volcanoes deposited precious minerals, such as copper, gold, and silver. The copper mine at Ajo is in the main vent of a large stratoform volcano that was once the size of Mount St. Helens.

After the Laramide Orogeny, the movement of the plates slowed, and the land was relatively quiet for about 20 million years. But then the North American plate sped up and, with a second sweep of its arm, again slid over part of the Farallon and Pacific plates, producing a second fury of volcanism, which rolled from east to west this time. Explosive eruptions from several volcanoes blanketed this region with ash and sloshed molten rhyolite and basalt across the land.

This was the mid-Tertiary Orogeny, which spanned the Southwest and lasted from 36 until 14 million years ago. It gave birth to the Basin and Range with the world's largest expanse of rhyolite. Molten rhyolite is chemically identical to molten granite, but it cools above the surface whereas granite forms below.

Most of the monument's mountains grew from this latest rage of volcanism. Several extinct volcanoes in the two-thousand-square-mile Ajo Volcanic Field fed these eruptions and flows. Diaz Spire, Diaz Peak, and Kino Peak are remnant necks of those old volcanoes. Less obvious volcanoes were atop the Cipriano Hills and the Batamote Mountains north of the monument. These

The arch, Arch canyon

Valley of the Ajo and Kino Peak, Bates Mountains

volcanoes showered the region with ash, which later compacted into tuff, and gushed molten basalt, rhyolite, and andesite.

The Batamote flow is the youngest of these lava flows, dating fourteen to sixteen million years past, and deepest, totaling over three hundred feet thick—with some individual flows measuring nearly fifty feet!

The most impressive geology of the monument is in the Ajo Range, which rises to 4,808 feet. This formidable volcanic wall is a series of tilted and tumbled horsts. Most of the rocks here—rhyolite, basalt, andesite, obsidian, quartz, feldspar, and mica—were formed when eruptions poured magma onto the surface.

Diaz Spire was a central volcanic pipe for the lighter colored rhyolite and, just east of Diaz Peak, a now-eroded vent was the likely source 18 million years ago of a thick bed of rhyolite's cousin, latite, which lies under the entire range. Twisted and folded bands of rhyolite can be seen on the Arch Canyon trail and in Bull Pasture. This rhyolite varies in thickness from 1,454 feet in Montezuma's Head to 2,208 feet at Mount Ajo. In some places, such as Bull Pasture and between Alamo and Estes Canyons, a thick layer of red-brown rhyolite meshes with lighter colored volcanic ash (tuff) and volcanic mudflows (lahars).

Tillotson Peak and the Diablo Mountains are massive horst blocks faulted away from the main Ajo range. Broad bands of tuff more than two hundred feet thick form the tan to yellowish layers visible in

Montezuma's Head, Ajo Mountains

Tillotson and the resistant cliffs of the Diablos. Since tuff is more porous and permeable than rhyolite, lichen frequently grows on it, giving the yellowish tuff cliffs a distinctive green patchwork.

Basalt, fast-moving lava that cools to weather-resistant rock, caps several of the monument's peaks, including Tillotson and Kino, slowing their erosion. Although basalt usually looks black, near the Diablo Canyon picnic area it has weathered to reddish brown. The Bates Mountains and their summit, the forbidding looking Kino Peak (3,197 feet), consist primarily of basalts from a volcanic neck reminiscent of Ship Rock in New Mexico.

The basaltic Pinacate lava shield southwest of the park dates from less than 3 million years ago. It resulted not from overriding plates or faulting, but from magma rising directly out of the deeper mantle itself in a plume like that which forms the islands of Hawaii.

Although the Growler Mountains lie mostly north of the monument in the Cabeza Prieta National Wildlife Refuge, they too are important to the monument's geological story. They consist of massive basalt flows and tuffs from a volcano at the southern end of the range. These flows dip gently eastward, but the west side of the range slices steeply in a series of cliffs and talus chutes. At the southern end of the Growlers we find some of the oldest (Precambrian and Paleozoic) rocks in Organ Pipe, as well as some of the monument's only metamorphosed sedimentary rock, such as marble. This area is

TOP: *Aguajita Wash with Cipriano Hills to right, Pinacate Peak on horizon*

BOTTOM: *Ajo Mountains*

Who's Thirsty?

If you want to live in a desert, you'd better have more than one strategy for getting a drink.

We humans are tied to canteens and spigots. In any season we require one to two gallons of water a day. Some animals are like us. They thrive in the desert, but they always know where to find a waterhole and can get to it daily. White-winged and mourning doves derive some of their water from cactus fruit, but they willingly fly up to twenty-five miles each way just to get a drink in the morning and another in the evening. White-tailed deer don't roam too far from water and need to drink every few days. This is why they hang around Bull Pasture, with its perennial water, but seldom are seen elsewhere in the monument. Some bats require regular drinks and at night they skim the surface of large pools.

However, other animals can take water or leave it. Desert bighorn sheep inhabit mountain ranges that may have no permanent water; they survive by eating juicy plants, including cacti, and by smart use of shade. If severely dehydrated, sheep can drink 20 percent of their body weight at one filling! Mule deer and javelina probably can survive on cactus and agave juices, but will drink one to two gallons per day if water is available. Sonoran prong-horn rarely have been observed drinking, indicating they can survive on moisture in their food.

Predators such as hawks, foxes, and coyotes can derive sufficient moisture from their prey, but they do hunt around waterholes and drink when water is available. Snakes, quail, roadrunners, Gila monsters, and desert tortoises are known to drink, but seldom have the chance. Kangaroo rats metabolize their own water from dried seeds. Even so, they have strategies to conserve water, such as staying cool in their dens at midday and rebreathing their moist breaths.

mineralized and saw active but financially marginal mining at the Yellow Jacket Mine and the Growler Mine. The big copper deposit at Ajo, mined since before recorded history, lies in quartz monzonite from the Laramide, but there is no monzonite in the monument.

The Puerto Blanco Mountains are faulted blocks of rhyolite and tuff, dating from 18 to 22 million years ago. The horizontal bedding of their darker rhyolite flows and yellowish tuff is clearly visible, especially in Pinkley Peak, the colorful 3,145 foot summit. In the western part of the Puerto Blancos, extensive thrusting and faulting cleaved a series of immense rock sheets stacked like sliced bread.

In this heavily fractured area, the Golden Bell Mine was worked hard by prospector Charlie Bell, but his ore assayed at only one-half ounce of gold for every ton of rock.

The prolonged ripping and tearing of the very earth itself challenges our comprehension, but the story continues today. Erosion, especially where faults have already fractured the rock, continues to fashion Organ Pipe's mountains and valleys. At Arch Canyon we see erosion's handiwork on a spectacular scale. Here an arch ninety feet wide by thirty-six feet tall opens to the skyline. Such arches and windows are formed on narrow ribs of rock by the expansion of freezing water or wet salt in cracks of the rock. Little by little the cracks are enlarged until pieces spall away and eventually open a window where this erosion pinches the middle of the cliff.

From a turn on the trail we look down on the graben valleys filled thousands of feet deep with sediment washed from the heights by ephemeral streams. As these streams slow, they drop their loads of rock, sand, and silt, forming fans of alluvium. These fans join one another and create *bajadas*, ramps from the steep slopes of the mountains to the flat valley floors where we'll camp tonight.

Geology provides the personal niches and challenges we find so enticing in the monument. Photographers focus on the picturesque canyons. Undaunted hikers scramble up arduous peaks, and children rally in a comfy granite cove for a game of hide-and-seek. Others of us wander into secluded canyons where outstretched arms can nearly touch both sides, or lunch beside a desert pool, watching reflections shimmer and doves drink. By dusk we reach camp and later, after hot food and glowing talk, we sleep on soft dreams of hard rock.

Tinaja in Alamo Canyon

Monkey flower growing from a seep

Visits to Organ Pipe are renowned for their vivid sunrises and sunsets. Dry and clean desert air scatters less white light than dirty or humid air, so more red light reaches our eyes unaffected by dust and unblocked by clouds. Distant volcanic eruptions may spew a layer of ash into the upper atmosphere reflecting sunlight after sunset and creating a memorable pinkish aura like the alpenglow of the high mountains. Also, because of the low latitude here, only about thirty-two degrees north, the sun slides beyond the horizon at a steeper angle than at higher latitudes, giving a shorter and brighter twilight, but also providing a wider celestial vision of both hemispheres.

Because of less haze and fewer lights in Organ Pipe than in a city, thirty times more stars are visible here with the unaided eye. The moon casts shadows, and the Milky Way has never seemed brighter. We can see earthshine on the crescent moon, planets look close enough to touch, and meteors blaze across the darkness. We can easily trace the classic constellation patterns of Scorpius and Orion. We are reminded why astronomy is a science for everyone and why world-famous Kitt Peak Observatory is only seventy miles east of us.

During the year, six of our other eight planets are visible to the unaided eye. Venus is the brightest planet when visible, showing as dawn's morning star or sunset's

Comet Hyakutake

evening star. Mars, Mercury, Jupiter, Saturn, and even Uranus may also be visible. With binoculars or a small telescope you can see Jupiter's four moons, Saturn's rings, and Neptune. For Pluto, that farthest and smallest of our planets, we need more sophisticated equipment.

The sky seems somehow different here, and glowing patches close to the horizon may puzzle us. The zodiacal light can be seen here every clear night for one and one-half hours after sunset and before sunrise. This faint, triangular glow of white light reflecting off dust, debris, and asteroids extends above the horizon from where the sun rises and where it sets. It is different from the electrical glow on the horizon from the region's cities. Above the northern horizon, exceptional sunspot activity may provide a rare show of the aurora borealis, whose dancing lights are seen from the monument every few years.

Splashed across the sky is the Milky Way, that spinning, spiral galaxy where we live. Shaped roughly like a discus with several spiraling arms, it is composed of billions of stars and is 100 thousand light years (30 trillion kilometers) across. What we see as diamonds strewn on black velvet is actually our view through the disk from our vantage in the Orion arm.

Comets and meteors blaze fiery paths across the black sky. Comets are interplanetary

Starlight, Star Bright

Ringtail atop saguaro

Sirius with constellation Canis Major

LEFT: *Scorpius, the scorpion constellation*

RIGHT: *The Big Dipper emerges*

bodies of ice and rock orbiting the sun. We see them from the earth as hanging lights, changing position from night to night. Organ Pipe was a popular place to watch the last appearance of Halley's Comet, which will be visible again in 2061.

Meteors, bits of space rocks and ice left by comets, plunge into the earth's atmosphere and burn as air friction melts them. What doesn't burn up, hits the earth. On any clear and dark night, observers can spot three to twenty meteors per hour. Meteor showers, such as August's Perseids or mid-November Leonids,

average fifty to sixty per hour, with rare shows dazzling us with 2,000 per *minute*!

Star watching is not only rewarding, it is relaxing, since it is best done from a chair or cot. Polaris, the North Star, can be found year round by aligning the Big Dipper or Cassiopeia. In winter, Orion, Ursus Major and Minor, and Sirius—the brightest star except the sun—draw our attention. In summer, Scorpius is obvious, down to the detail of its stinger, with our attention also drawn to Sagittarius, the Summer Triangle, and orange-red Arcturus, the fourth brightest star.

In spring Canopus lies low on the southern horizon, flickering like an airplane. Being part of constellation Carina, Canopus is out of sight for most areas of the United States, but we can see it at Organ Pipe. The Andromeda galaxy and the Orion Nebula also fascinate viewers here.

Many of these sky features can be seen from the campground and the amphitheater, but some visitors prefer to set up their telescopes along the two-way section of the Ajo Mountain Loop road or at Alamo campground. Only the howling of a coyote and the flutter of a nighthawk remind us that we're not aboard some spaceship hurtling through the heavens. On second thought, they do remind us that we *are...* on Starship Earth.

As one park visitor remarked, "Plants by day and planets by night.

Lights Out

On Organ Pipe's horizon we can see the glow from distant cities as well as nearby towns. Lights from Phoenix, Sonoyta, Tucson, and even Los Angeles compete with stars. This computer-enhanced chart depicts those photometric changes and confirms what our eyes tell us. Some communities around the world encourage citizens to reduce light pollution by shading outdoor lights and using special bulbs. Thirty times more stars are visible from Organ Pipe than in a city, but, as more people move to the Southwest, this may decline unless we take precautions to insure our dark skies. Hold the chart overhead to simulate a night sky.

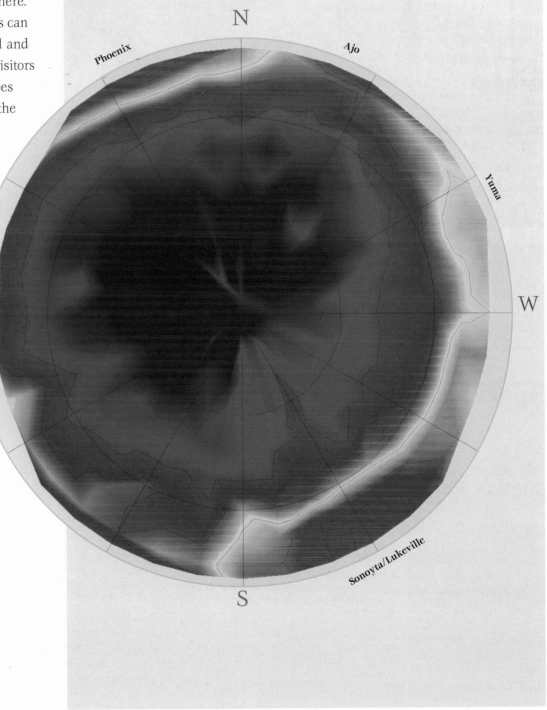

A canopy of velvet mesquites soften the glare and heat behind us. Leaves, fallen from a regal Fremont cottonwood, crackle underfoot as we walk. We're startled by flapping wings as a green heron lifts out of the thicket ahead. Tracks of mule deer punch the path's soft ground. Moats of bulrush, sedges, and a few Goodding willows surround a pond. Dainty fruit trees from Spanish colonial days hide among the forest. Desert hackberry, graythorn, lycium, and condalia attract a host of berry-eating birds like verdins and phainopeplas. At sunset bats wheel over the pond to drink. We realize this must be a magical place.

The springs at Quitobaquito perfectly fit our image of a desert oasis: dense foliage, impressive trees, pools of clear and ever-welling water, ancient fields, and a hub for wayfarers then as now. Quitobaquito is all of these.

Known to the O'odham people as ʻAʻal Waipia (Little Wells), the springs now number two reliable ones, with a half dozen more appearing at will and revealed only by the verdancy above them. The O'odham have camped here since there have been O'odham, as did their ancestors and theirs before. Quitobaquito was on the trail to everywhere. For ancients and moderns alike, this spot has been a paradise in an otherwise baked and thirsty land.

Wildlife, too, have found sanctuary here. Herons, killdeer, and ducks

Quitobaquito

rest on their seasonal flights. White-throated swifts, black phoebes, and purple martins live here year round. Most species of mammals in the monument have been seen here at one time or another, and nearly half of the monument's plants are represented nearby.

And fish. Fish? Yes, Quitobaquito is home to a special species of pupfish, the *Cyprinodon macularius eremus*. If we stand quietly on the bank, we see them dart past or fin idly in the current of the canal. They are captives, held by time and circumstance when the Sonoyta River meandered south. This pool is their universe.

Their thumb-size, rounded bodies sport narrow, dark sidebars. Males are blue on top, while the females and juveniles are silver-sided with tan or olive on their backs. Their population rapidly expands or falls to fit food and water conditions. In good times they may number eight thousand, but they decline to half that in leaner days.

Pupfish prefer the shallow water of springs, streams, and marshes. They can tolerate high salinity, high temperatures, and low amounts of dissolved oxygen, conditions which would

Springs and Things

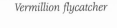

Vermillion flycatcher

Ruddy duck

Quitobaquito at dusk

but the pond varies from 62 to 106 degrees. The water mixes daily and is less salty than seawater.

Pupfish are far better at surviving physical extremes than competing with other fish or predators. They have been wiped out in other ponds by catfish, shiners, and dace. These Quitobaquito pupfish are the only natural population in Arizona. Their subspecies name, *eremus*, means solitary—the last of the line— though a few artificial colonies have been established elsewhere from Quitobaquito stock.

Pupfish originally lived throughout the Southwest in rivers, streams, and lakes. They even lived in the upper Gulf of California, the Colorado River, and the now dry Lake Manly, which once covered part of Death Valley. As the waters receded after the last glacial period, pockets of pupfish were left behind in headwater springs and feeder streams. Each surviving group then evolved to fit to its changing surroundings; pupfish breed quickly, so generations may quickly adapt. Pupfish in Quitobaquito may even be different than ones still struggling in the intermittent Sonoyta River, a quarter mile south of the pond.

Pupfish hatch from eggs a few days after deposition and may live as long as three years, although most survive only a year. They eat a variety of small aquatic animals and plants. They share their world here with Sonoran mud turtles (*Kinosternon sonoriense*), small, round-shelled turtles found in many rivers and streams of the Southwest. You may see one glide past as you watch pupfish.

kill other fish. Individuals can survive in water up to 111 degrees Fahrenheit and as low as 45 degrees, though they prefer water less than 104 degrees. They can tolerate oxygen concentrations as low as one-seventieth normal running water. And, they can cope with salinity ranging from that of distilled water to three times as salty as the ocean.

Today the fish in Quitobaquito don't face such extremes. Water coming from the spring itself is usually 78 to 83 degrees Fahrenheit

The Quitobaquito pond attracts one of the United States' two known populations of Underwood's mastiff bats (*Eumops underwoodi*), which come here to snatch insects above the pond and to skim a drink from the wide surface. The pocketed free-tailed bat (*Nyctinomops femorosacca*) also drinks at the pond.

Legends still are whispered of monstrous and evil *carbuncos,* which ate people and thrashed the water in anger at a similar oasis spring, Quitovac, thirty miles southeast of here. Scoffers would do well to remember the massive mammoth bones found near that spring. Quitobaquito would have been mammoth habitat, too, but no bones have yet been excavated here. Today the venerable Quitovac is on the decline, being pumped and bulldozed for farming and mining.

Quitobaquito springs are fed by an underground aquifer on the western edge of La Abra Plain. About 10 percent of the precipitation flowing southward off the Cipriano Hills and the Puerto Blanco Mountains percolates into the bajada and valley sediments that overlie bedrock. It seeps down to the water table lying fifteen to one hundred feet below the surface and then flows southward toward the Sonoyta River. As the water nears the international border it encounters the granite bedrock of the Quitobaquito Hills. Since the land northeast of the hills is up to fifty feet higher than the south side, pressure forces water to the surface through fractures in the granite, where it gurgles forth at several springs and seeps. Quitobaquito Springs is the largest of

these, with a flow of twenty to forty gallons per minute. Aguajita, Burro, Muddy, and Williams are smaller springs in the same system. Their water has traveled below the surface for two thousand years before reappearing.

Some European settlers brought domesticated plants to the springs. We can still see pomegranate and fig trees. The fig trees (*Ficus carica*) may be from stock or seed brought in 1698 by Padre Kino, so it is often called mission fig. They are so delicious that few ripen before birds devour them. Also here are pomegranates (*Punica granatum*). These too may be from Padre Kino's stock, or at least from cuttings he cultivated in Quitovac or Sonoyta. Their sweet fruits ripen in summer. The Fremont cottonwoods are not native either, but probably are cuttings brought from one tree, since all of the cottonwoods at the pond and in the Sonoyta valley are unpollinated females.

The tree caper (*Atamisquea emarginata*) is not found anywhere else in the United States. A small tree with white flowers and red fruit, it is home to Howarth's white butterfly (*Ascia howarthi*), which

lays its eggs only in tree caper. Its larvae feed on nothing else, but adults may take nectar from wolfberry and bebbia. Adults are difficult to spot, since they usually fly within the canopy of mesquite thickets.

The pond area bustles with other insects. At least fifty species of butterflies and skippers can be found during the year. And, seventeen species of grasshoppers and katydids live here, including a grasshopper (*Leptysma hebardi*) that lives exclusively on cattails.

There are other important springs in the monument, but none compare to the oasis we enjoy at Quitobaquito.

Green heron

TOP LEFT: *Quitobaquito desert pupfish*

Slogging across the sandy flat, we snake around creosote bushes, cholla, and rodent burrows. We yearn to touch the past. We daydream of great walls, cliff houses, and pyramids, so we're disappointed to see only creosote. We see no signs of people. What good could this barren place have been to anyone?

Ahead the flat is pinched by arroyos converging to rush headlong through a breach in the basalt mountains. We walk on, hoping for shade. Then, at our feet, a cobble of basalt pushes out of the sand and looks somehow out of place. It is. We kneel for a closer look. Faint in the sand are pottery sherds, bits of seashell, and a trail made by many feet. But whose? We drop our packs and wonder.

Much of the Sonoran Desert's treasures of human occupation lie on or near the surface, meaning that once any artifact is disturbed or removed, the fragile pattern of the picture is blurred or smashed. We leave the pieces where we found them, but we begin to see.

Organ Pipe country has long been a lively place and has a rich story to tell. With only 2.5 percent of the monument archaeologically surveyed, already four hundred ancient sites have been recorded. People have lived in Organ Pipe for at least twelve thousand years, probably longer. Here they found food, water, and shelter, and here they stayed. Their origins, identities, and histories remain unclear and

Bedrock metates and chuparosa

subject to much archeological study and interpretation.

Not much is known about the earliest humans, the Malpais people. They left stone tools, but no pottery. They left trails and clearings where they camped, but no buildings. They left rock-ringed circles and ninety-foot-long intaglio ground-figures of lizards, but little else. Their tools have been covered with microbial varnish, and their seashells have grayed with age. Most things they used have long since turned to dust. Other peoples, including us, have followed their trails and camped in their clearings. Just when the Malpais people arrived here is open to scholarly discussion, but some archaeologists contend that the Malpais arrived at least forty thousand years ago, having migrated on early crossings of the Bering Strait between Siberia and Alaska.

Twelve thousand years ago this was pinyon, oak, and juniper country, with yuccas and grasses across the valleys. Animals included mammoths and saber-toothed tigers. While the Malpais still were living here, bands of Paleoindians moved into the region. They hunted game and gathered fruit, seeds, and roots, but they too left little evidence of their stay, and nothing is known of their customs or language.

The Malpais and the Paleo-indians were from two larger groups whose ranges overlap here in the monument. From the west came the San Dieguito people, whose territory centered around the San Dieguito River in southern California.

A Frontier and Beyond

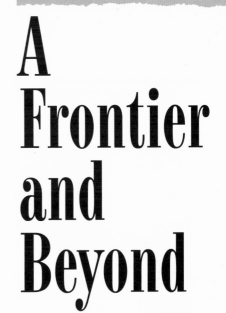

Clovis point

Hohokam projectile points such as these have been found in the monument

Incised petroglyphs near Kino Peak

Petroglyphs against desert varnish

They left us evidence of stone tools, but likely they also used tools of wood and bone. From the east came the Clovis people, remembered for their distinctive spear points used to slay mammoths.

About ten thousand years ago, as the climate warmed and the desert marched northward, tools and artifacts began to change. These innovations may have been brought by new groups of people, the Amargosans, or may have been the results of changing technologies among people who spoke the same language. This archaeological period, called the Archaic, lasted sporadically until A.D. 300. These folk left stone tools, projectile points, and obsidian knives. Sometimes they lived in shallow rock caves in the mountains, made simple shelters of brush and hides, or simply camped in the open. Here again, there seem to be two overlapping cultures: the Cochise Culture, centered in southeastern Arizona, and the Amargosan Culture, based in southeastern California.

The Archaic peoples had an extensive trade network. They swapped items across hundreds of miles, including turquoise from northeastern Arizona, abalone shell from the Pacific Ocean, and salt and seashells from the Gulf of California. They carried forty-pound basalt boulders tens of miles from mountain quarries to valley camps for use as rock-bowl *metates* in which to grind seeds and beans. They filled gourd canteens from pools of rainwater in the mountains. They left grinding holes in the bedrock near tinajas. Like their predecessors, these Archaic people appear to have been small groups of wanderers.

About A.D. 300 the culture changed again. Group sizes grew, campsites became permanent. People made pottery, dug wells, and trenched canals. Still they hunted and gathered, but increasingly they relied on cultivated crops. In the creosote flats archaeologists have found villages two hundred acres in size. These settlements centered around a community well, hand dug at a time when the water table was closer to the surface. Their houses were made of brush dabbed with mud or draped with hide. A half-mile-long canal in the monument reminds us of their farming.

Their villages were organized. They had special areas for carving seashells into tools and jewelry. They had areas for chipping stone tools from raw rock brought miles from quarry sites. They had areas for molding and firing pottery. They had garbage dumps for their spent tools, broken pottery, and bones burned in cooking. They almost left real fingerprints, too, with caring hand-marks on pottery. In one case, rock rubble outlines the thighs and hips of the person who sat and chipped stone tools at a quarry site. It's as though they were here yesterday instead of centuries ago.

These settlers were a mix of *Hohokam, Patayan,* and *Trincheras,* three cultures intertwined by trade, society, and geography. The Patayan people were from the Colorado River valley. They farmed in flood plains, and they made pottery. They exchanged deer hides, stone tools, and arrowheads with the people

O'odham women near the turn of the century

Building a Tohono O'odham dwelling, called a "ki"

around them. The Trincheras people, from lands south and east of the monument, were farmers who built fortified observation hills, farmed terraces above the valleys, and produced distinctive purple-on-red Trincheras pottery.

The Hohokam who lived here were affiliated with those who farmed the Salt River valley of Phoenix, irrigating with two hundred miles of hand-dug canals. Between 1358 and 1382 ravaging floods poured down the Salt River, washing out the headgates of their canals. The flood deepened the river channel, and the entire canal system was left high and dry. Drought and famine followed. By 1450 their civilization in the Salt River valley had disintegrated, and when the first Spanish explorers visited the valley, no one was home. But what became of them?

Hohokam long have been thought to have disappeared. Some translate their name itself as meaning "people gone." But growing evidence shows that their descendants are still here. Rousted by famine and by civil war, the Hohokam had fled the Salt River Valley and dispersed across southern Arizona and northern Sonora, including the open desert and valleys of Organ Pipe.

O'odham sacred legend may report this upheaval. Once there was a great, great flood on the land. Creator of the O'odham, *I'itoi*, was saved by floating in a jar made from creosote gum. He landed on Pinacate Peak, southwest of the monument. There I'itoi and his collaborator, Coyote, created many living things including people, who multiplied too fast and made problems. So I'itoi waved his arms, caused another great flood, and stayed in the Pinacate from four to four hundred years. When the land dried, I'itoi returned north with his people, the O'odham, who chased away others living on their land. The O'odham are still here today and celebrate these events in the annual ceremony of the Vigida.

A northern O'odham group became the *Pima* Indians (the *Akimel* or River People), and two southern groups became the Papago Indians, now known as the *Tohono O'odham* (Desert or Country People), and the *Hia-ced O'odham* (People of the Sand). These three groups of Hohokam adopted different lifestyles based on their seasonal needs to hunt and harvest, and on their access to water. The Pima, who lived in permanent settlements along the perennial Gila River, could farm and hunt from one village. The Tohono O'odham, who settled in the Ajo Mountains and eastward, lived in villages or farms near ponds, wells, and springs during the winter. They made houses of mesquite poles covered by saguaro ribs and ocotillo wands. Sometimes mud was slapped on the walls and roof. Brush dams across small arroyos diverted water to irrigate temporary fields (*temporales*), and the style of farming was called *ak chiñ*. Their crops included corn, chiltepin peppers, amaranth, melons, and tepary beans. In summer they migrated to mountain camps, where they lived under *ramadas* while hunting game and harvesting cactus fruit and mesquite beans.

The Hia-Ced O'odham lived west

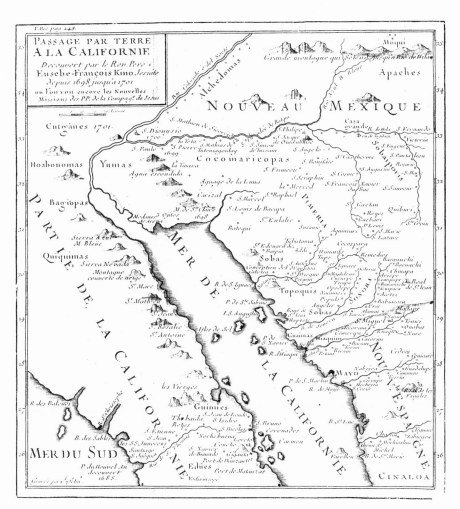

Padre Eusebio Kino's 1701 map of the Organ Pipe region

of the Ajo Mountains, especially around Quitobaquito and in the Pinacate region of Mexico. They found water in tinajas and springs, harvested cactus fruit, and hunted lizards, deer, and bighorn sheep. They also gathered the tubers of sand root and beans from mesquite and paloverde trees. Their harvests and hunts followed the seasons, so they had few permanent camps.

The Akimel, Tohono, and Hia-Ced O'odham prospered by living *with* the desert. They blended with its seasons, treated it gently, and listened to its moods. In this century O'odham have lived at Quitobaquito, Armenta Well, and Bates Well. Today they live in communities around the monument, but still visit it for ceremonies and to gather traditional foods.

When Europeans arrived they brought new technologies, foods, and ways. They introduced metallurgy, cows, and writing. The first expedition into Organ Pipe country was probably in 1540 when Melchior Díaz, a captain in Coronado's expedition, came through on his way to the mouth of the Colorado River. Others followed sporadically.

Eusebio Kino, a Jesuit Padre, came to Sonoyta in 1698. He planned to christianize the local Indians and hoped to find a land route to the Jesuit missions in Baja and Alta California. Kino followed ancient trails well known to his O'odham guides. He brought with him three dozen head of cattle,

Then and Now

The desert may seem eternal and unchanging, but evidence shows many changes. Cameras started recording Organ Pipe's scenery as early as 1896 with Army Captain David. D. Gaillard and the boundary survey team. By relocating the original photo site, we can take a photo today and compare what has changed—or what has not changed—since that first shot.

Researchers can "read" the vegetation and ground to determine plant ages, species changes, and erosion rates. By knowing the temperature and precipitation requirements for the plants in the picture, scientists can track subtle changes in the climate, which seems to be warming and drying. Arizona's mean temperature has risen 3 degrees Fahrenheit since 1870.

The first photo, taken in 1956, looks north along the loop drive at the crest of the Ajo Mountains and shows organ pipes, saguaros, foothill paloverdes, triangle leaf bursages, jumping chollas, and ocotillos.

The second was taken in 1980 at the same place. The main organ pipe cactus is easily recognizable, even though it grew taller and sprouted sixteen new arms in the interlude. Several of the saguaros are now taller, but one-third of them have died. Chollas are fewer—the largest one in 1956 is a skeleton in 1980—but the bursages persist.

These photos show that changes have indeed occurred in the last century. The most dramatic changes have taken place where cattle no longer graze; trampled areas around major springs are slowly regaining communities of native plants. Other areas now have more saguaros or more grasses, while some sites show declines of saguaros and increases in trees and shrubs.

Some changes continue to threaten the monument. Fire is one of them. Few plants of the Sonoran Desert are adapted to survive intense fire. When fires suddenly sweep dried grasses, cactus and trees likely will die. The photograph of a human-caused burn near Gachado Well in 1983 shows the immediate damage, and comparative annual photographs monitor the sequence of new plants. However, it will take decades before the cactus and trees return.

grains, and new ideas for self-sustaining missions. Before he arrived, the O'odham grew maize and tepary beans, and supplemented their diet with native animals and plants. Kino introduced a number of extras into their larders—wheat, peas, grapes, watermelon, onions, figs, and cabbage, as well as chickens and goats. In time these became staples across the region.

Kino made a number of trips throughout the region and provided some of the first written records of routes and places. On one of his excursions Kino climbed Pinacate Peak in Mexico, which he named *Volcán de Santa Clara*. As he gazed westward he was startled to see the Colorado delta, a revelation that contradicted those geographers and sailors of the day who thought the Gulf of California extended so far north that California was an island. Kino announced, *"California no es una isla,"* and drew a new map of the region.

Kino founded a mission at Sonoyta in 1701, but it was abandoned five years later. Padre Heinrich Ruhen re-established it in 1751, but later that year the O'odham rebelled against the Spanish occupation of their land, killed Ruhen, and destroyed the mission. It was over fifty years before immigrants from the interior of Mexico again rolled through the Sonoyta River Valley. They were soldiers, settlers, and families bound for the presidios of San Diego, Los Angeles, and even San Francisco. In 1849 word reached the world that gold had been discovered at Sutter's Mill in California. Thousands of people in Mexico heard the call of riches and headed westward. The route went from Hermosillo, to Caborca, to Sonoyta, then Yuma and on to California. Many of these travelers stopped by Quitobaquito Springs for water. Some, unprepared and unknowing, ventured into the desert in summer. As many as four hundred died along the way. Later the difficult route became known as *El Camino del Diablo*, the Devil's Highway.

With the Gadsden Purchase in 1853 the area of what is now the monument became United States territory, and with the change came Americans. One of the first American settlers was Andrew Dorsey, who arrived at Quitobaquito Springs in 1861. He set up a store to trade with the Mexicans and O'odham already living there and with travelers on the trail to Yuma. He dammed the largest springs and made a pond with irrigation ditches feeding fields for his crops.

In 1886 a now obscure settler, W. B. Bates, dug a well where groundwater of Growler Wash is pushed toward the surface by rock below. Bates sold the well and ranch to Ruben Daniels in 1917. Later John McDaniels and then Henry Gray owned it. Mexicans called Bates's well *El Veit*. The Hia-Ced O'odham knew it as *Juñi Ka:c* (Place of the Saguaro Jam), because the saguaros here produced exceptional fruit for making jam. The well also was a main watering stop on a wagon road from Ajo to Yuma.

The region remained a frontier into the twentieth century. Bandits, scientists, ranchers, miners, laborers, patriots, and drifters mingled in

these unsettled times on this restless frontier. Pancho Villa sympathizers hid in Bull Pasture from Carranza troops. As recently as 1917 Villa bandits held up a delivery car between Ajo and Sonoyta, and in 1918 three *Villistas* were executed in Sonoyta.

Residents of the region eked out livings from small-time commerce, mining, ranching, and odd jobs. Local news touted the opening of a new shop or the birth of a colt.

Growler Mine, about 1940

"Getting by" was the order of the day. A marginal well called the Needmore could serve as a symbol for the history of the region: need more water, need more cows, need more range, need more everything. Settlers fell into two categories— very desperate or very optimistic. The rest were born here and stayed.

Their history reads more like footnotes than full chapters. Pat Dowling built a mill and a few buildings along the border in the late 1800s. Later this outpost became the official customs-house until a new port of entry was opened about 1915. John Growler and Frederick Wall found ore and dug wells at the north end of the Ajo Mountains. Jeff Milton, famous lawman, patrolled the border from Sonoyta to Yuma looking for illegal activities. But he also had to act as doctor, guide, and miner.

Francisco "Pancho" Villa, whose sympathizers hid out in Bull Pasture

RIGHT: *Jeff Milton, lawman*

World War I aviator Lieutenant Frank Luke was the pride and sorrow of the border in 1918. Luke worked in the copper mine at Ajo before his enlistment, his brother once lived in Ajo, and the family had property along the border at what is now known as Lukeville. His family received word that "Frank destroyed two balloons and one airplane today. Now credited with downing eleven balloons and four airplanes." Six weeks later Luke was reported missing in action. Posthumously he was awarded the Congressional Medal of Honor.

Cipriano Ortega's hacienda at Santo Domingo, southeast of Quitobaquito, 1907

There were a number of mineral claims in the area, but few of them proved profitable. Most were hobbies, dreams, or schemes. The experience of Andrew Belcher Gray was typical. While surveying a possible transcontinental railroad route near Sonoyta, he purchased forty pounds of copper ore "represented to yield gold of great value; but from an analysis of a specimen, it exhibited no such indicators."

Two mines may have paid for themselves. These were the Growler west of Bates Well and the Victoria near Senita Basin. Other claims and digs were exercises in optimism, and

most of them changed hands often and without paydays.

The Victoria Mine originally went by the name *La Americana*. That's when Cipriano Ortega owned it. He was a Mexican citizen, but the mine was in the United States, where he had worked it since the 1880s. Silver was the main product, accompanied by some gold, copper, and lead. A wandering prospector and his wife had originally found it, but had turned it over to Ortega, a highwayman who accumulated cattle, mining claims, a ranch, and eventually a degree of respectability. He even had a steam-driven grinding mill at his hacienda, Santo Domingo, on the Sonoyta River southeast of Quitobaquito. A subsequent owner, Mikul Levy, claimed that Ortega had taken some $80,000 in ore from the mine, but Levy didn't guess how much Ortega had invested.

Levy acquired the mine in 1899 and renamed it the Victoria, after the wife of his store clerk. Levy deepened the shaft in search of more ore, but at 312 feet the vein ran below the water table and without the money to buy giant pumps, Levy was unable to continue. After that a series of partners and owners participated in futile attempts to resurrect the diggings. A boarding house, kitchen bunk house, blacksmith shop, storehouse, two adobe buildings, and a large tent were set up. But an engineer estimated it would take another $75,000 to tunnel to the main ore vein. The price of silver stayed low, and the price of timbers rose. Other claims were filed on nearby land and some promising ore found, but profits never met expenses. The area wasn't even active enough to become a mining district. A caretaker was hired to watch the inactive diggings until Levy died in 1941.

The Growler Mine and its neighbor, the Yellow Jacket, didn't fare much better. At one time there were twenty-six patented claims in the district and three headframes for hoists, but the entire mining district produced only six tons of copper, two ounces of gold, and two hundred ounces of silver. Total production value? Two thousand dollars. Prospectors and investors hoped for another bonanza like the rich copper find at Ajo, but the geology just wasn't as generous. Even the best of mines had petered out before the monument was established, and for virtually all of the prospectors and miners their claims were part-time jobs.

Victoria Leon, namesake of the Victoria Mine, 1968

LEFT: *Frank Luke*

What's in a Name?

If something is important in this borderland of three languages, you can bet it will have several names. Some names are distinct, but others originated in one language and were adopted by the others. Jojoba, for example, originally was an O'odham word.

ENGLISH	SPANISH	O'ODHAM
organ pipe	pitahaya dulce	cucuvis
saguaro	sahuaro	ha:sañ
senita	sinita	ce:mi
bighorn sheep	borrego cimarrón	tjúrsa, cusoiñ
pronghorn	berrendo	ku'wid
jojoba	jojova	hohovai

But, common names of plants and animals in even one language can confuse us. Sage is such. Writer Zane Gray saw our creosote and called it "sagebrush," but creosote really is in the family of caltrops while sagebrush is grouped with sunflowers. Others call creosote "greasewood," but greasewood properly applies to a goosefoot, *Sarcobatus vermiculatus*, which thrives in the Mojave Desert but not around here.

This desert does have a sagebrush, *Artemisia ludoviciana*, whose leaves smell kitchen-good when crushed, but neither it nor our *Ambrosia*-genus bursages are true sages. Real sages, botanically speaking, are salvias and have the square stem of the mint family. In springtime the monument has *Salvia columbariae*, an honest-to-goodness sage known as chia.

Besides mining, ranching was the other primary industry here. In the early 1900s several settlers followed the dream of a little ranch of their own. A retired cavalry scout from the Apache War raised a few goats and cows and dug a well in a canyon now called Estes, after him. Other settlers dug and drilled wells like the Blankenship, Acuña, and Bonita. It never was good range, but with ample troughs of water a few cattle could make it. A cattleman's range handbook for 1926 rated this land at "very low carrying capacity," and noted that its forage was primarily mesquite leaves and beans, with short-lived annuals occasionally furnishing feed for a few weeks.

The best known cattleman in Organ Pipe was Robert Louis Gray (1875-1962). Born in Arkansas, he came to Arizona by way of Texas, where he learned the ways of cowboying. In 1919 he packed his family into a Model-T Ford and a covered wagon, and herded his cattle to the Blankenship Ranch. He and his family worked hard and, as neighbors found they couldn't make a living from cattle, the Gray's bought their spreads. His brand was the E Bar, and at one time he owned virtually all of the ranches and wells in the monument. Dos Lomitas was the ranch headquarters, with line camps at Blankenship, Gachado, Alamo, Pozo Nuevo, Bonita, and Bates wells. In this unsparing desert it took land as vast as the five hundred square mile monument to sustain one ranching family. More than one head of cattle per square mile overgrazed the range, which is still trying to renew itself after fifty years of hard grazing.

The Grays did not ride the range as depicted in cowboy lore. Instead they waited for the cattle to come to water troughs at the wells and captured them at corrals with a one-way trap gate. Cattle were then trucked to market. This greatly reduced the need for line riders and roundups, but it also intensified the impact of cattle. The Gray's first permit was for 550 head, but they contested that and it was raised to 1,050. When the Gray family cattle were finally trucked off for the last time, inspectors counted more than seventeen hundred. The Grays were the last family to ranch in the monument. In his last days Robert still slept under a tin roof, drank from a tin cup, and rode his horse to town.

Nomads, villagers, growers, miners, ranchers, tourists: each and all tried to shape the land to their visions and dreams, but this is a hard, reluctant desert. Most efforts have been in vain. The scars remain of overgrazed land, barren mines, and roads to nowhere. A stressed desert is slow to heal. Those did best who tried to live with the land, not against it. They let the land shape them. Remaining to be seen is how the hand of our generation will rest upon this special place.

Erosion caused by too many cattle on fragile range

Robert Gray's eldest son, Henry, about 1972 at Bates Well

Only 10 percent of Organ Pipe's visitors are lucky enough to come in summer. The rest don't know what they're missing! Summer is prime time. Up in Alaska, a newcomer is called a *cheechako* until surviving a winter. In this deep desert of Organ Pipe, no one's a full-fledged "desert rat" until spending the summer.

After the spring annuals have flowered, seeded, and wilted, and after most visitors have gone home, this desert gets serious. The vivid yellows of the paloverde trees in late April announce the end of spring and the advent of summer. The blue paloverde blooms first, setting clouds of bright flowers along the washes. Then the foothill paloverdes blanket the slopes with the glory of their yellow petals. Giant saguaros and majestic organ pipes flower and fruit. It's so good here that doves fly from southern Mexico just to line up for the feast.

In May patches of pink appear across the valleys, subtle at first then profuse like cherry blossoms. Usually staid ironwood trees burst with a million flowers. Their gray-green hue subtly shifts to pink-lavender as they trade leaves for flowers. Large rings of yellow flowers crown burly barrel cacti, while lavender patches of petite mammillaria petals peek from under bursages.

In June, when the weather is hottest, the smoke tree pours forth masses of tiny indigo flowers which

Owl's clover and Mexican gold poppies, remnants of spring

set orange-dotted green seeds. It gets its name from its ethereal and usually leafless shape, which at a distance resembles not wood but smoke rising from the sands. In the mountains white masses of Arizona rosewood spread across the slopes. Agave, too, blooms then, sending up tall stalks of yellow panicles to be pollinated by bats and bees.

Summer also rewards our vigil with the flowering of the night-blooming cereus, also known as the queen-of-the-night cactus. Even for tough-hided desert rats the experience borders on mystical rapture. The queen usually grows hidden within creosote bushes, and its slender stems belie the huge underground tuber which sustains it through drought. It blooms only one night a year, opening at sundown and closing shortly after sunrise. But oh what a night!

The bud slowly opens into a pure white flower four inches wide, one of the largest flowers in the monument. The clarity of its whiteness, visible hundreds of feet away, attracts moths, especially the white-lined sphinx moth (*Hyles lineata*). All of the buds on a plant bloom the same night, in tune with most plants in the vicinity, to insure cross-pollination.

But, unlike most cactus flowers, which have no scent, it is the queen's perfume that is most memorable. Some describe it as musky sandalwood, or delectable delight. Some simply say it is ineffable. But once experiencing its ambrosial scent, we're never the same again. It's like knowing one of Nature's very deepest secrets.

Summer Sun

Giant hairy desert scorpion

Dust Devils and Monsoons

Dust devils, not tumbleweeds, should be a symbol of the West. Some days we can see a dozen at once spinning their way across the creosote plains, twirling dust and leaves aloft. Viewing is especially good in springtime from any vantage point overlooking the monument's four valleys: La Abra Plain, Growler Valley, Valley of the Ajo, and Sonoyta River valley.

Like mini-tornados, dust devils are caused by differential heating. They start from hot spots on the ground, especially beds of dry arroyos, and their thermal updrafts spiral skyward. Once born, they seemingly wander with minds of their own, and about half rotate clockwise while the rest spin counterclockwise. Most form between 11 A.M. and 4 P.M., with the largest growing in early afternoon. Devils may be hundreds of feet wide and, as sailplane pilots have discovered, may extend upward to fifteen thousand feet. Although they may twirl for a hour, most last fewer than three minutes.

The most violent and impressive winds, though, arrive with summer monsoon thunderstorms, along with frequent lightning, reverberating thunder, and deluges of rain. Thunderstorms are not novel to most monument visitors, but their aftermath may be. Intense downpour onto hard ground produces high runoff. A sheet of water inches deep pours across thousands of acres of land and races downslope, scouring the ground. When it reaches arroyos, it thunders along in a torrential flash flood. Trees rip out of the ground, tons of mud pile in new places, and puddles in silty lowlands hold water for a couple of weeks, long enough for Couch's spadefoot toads to produce a new generation. These storms turn tame road crossings into dangerous maelstroms for several hours and remind us to "Stop, look, and listen" before crossing dips in the rainy season. Few sights are more impressive than Kuakatch or Alamo Wash in roaring flood.

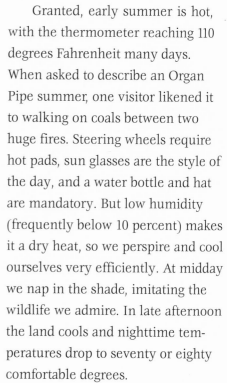

Granted, early summer is hot, with the thermometer reaching 110 degrees Fahrenheit many days. When asked to describe an Organ Pipe summer, one visitor likened it to walking on coals between two huge fires. Steering wheels require hot pads, sun glasses are the style of the day, and a water bottle and hat are mandatory. But low humidity (frequently below 10 percent) makes it a dry heat, so we perspire and cool ourselves very efficiently. At midday we nap in the shade, imitating the wildlife we admire. In late afternoon the land cools and nighttime temperatures drop to seventy or eighty comfortable degrees.

Rains start in mid-July or August. For several weeks clouds build with moisture pulled from the Gulf of Mexico or the Pacific Ocean. Humidity rises; days are sultry. But then one afternoon puffy clouds percolate into a towering thunderhead. Dust spins ahead of the fast moving curtain of water and lightning strokes the sky while tents billow and chairs tumble. The scent of creosote and the sound of thunder refresh our senses. Rain and hail pummel the ground, and those usually dry washes flow bank to bank, proving their names. Later a double rainbow may arc the eastern sky.

These monsoon rains and heat bring an array of annual flowers not seen during the spring. This summer crop is less flashy than spring, but orange caltrops and stands of yellow devil's claw splash the countryside. Pungent scent from yellow pectis flowers drifts on the air. Perennial plants swing into action, too. In springtime they coast on winter's rain and devote themselves to flowering and seeding. With the summer rains, they dedicate themselves to serious growing.

Animals too are most alive in summer. Gambel's quail chicks hatch as walnut-sized fluffs seemingly blessed with wheels. Their feet are blurs as they race to keep up with their strolling parents. Awkward young doves follow their parents to water; brown-crested flycatchers feed their squawking offspring. The nubs of horns sprout on bighorn lambs. Toad eggs hatch, growing to tadpoles within days and into hopping toads within two weeks. Kangaroo rats and pocket mice scurry looking for seeds to store, while snakes stalk them in the cool of evening. At night millipedes roam the ground grazing the cryptobiotic crust. There's a frenzy and purpose to it all. It's as if everyone and everything is shouting, "We're alive! We're alive!"

Our eyes are heavy with slumber on a sultry afternoon. We doze, but we don't forget these dreams of desert. We have seen it white hot and crystal bright. And we hear echoes of ancient Zeno reminding us, "When we have provided against hunger, cold, and thirst, all else is luxury." An Organ Pipe summer is a luxury of the most memorable and priceless kind.

CLOCKWISE FROM TOP LEFT:
Night-blooming cereus, spadefoot toad, summer thunderstorm over Ajo Mountains, flash flood

A flash of white spins ahead, turning broadside in our path. It pauses for an instant and then blurs as puffs of dust mark its sprint. It's gone in a blink. We've just met this desert's fleetest animal, the Sonoran pronghorn, *Antilocapra americana sonoriensis*. There are fewer than five hundred of these magnificent but endangered mammals. They can sprint at forty miles an hour for several miles, and an individual's home may extend across hundreds of square miles. As might be expected of such wanderers, they refuse to stay within the monument's protection. They just don't stay put. They know food, friends, and home; they don't know boundary lines.

They symbolize why Organ Pipe Cactus National Monument is this region's first Biosphere Reserve, an international designation for protected areas of worldwide importance where park managers and neighboring residents work together regionally to ensure the futures of those wild creatures that can't stay within the lines. The United Nations Educational, Scientific, and Cultural Organization (UNESCO) sponsors these cooperative projects.

In the early 1930s, enlightened leaders and concerned citizens worried that priceless desert jewels would be lost, and they set about to save them. The organ pipe cactus, desert bighorn sheep, saguaro cactus, Joshua tree yucca, and desert palm headed the list. In 1937, after much discussion, President Franklin

Organ pipe cactus at dusk

D. Roosevelt signed Organ Pipe Cactus National Monument into existence, helping save the organ pipe, desert bighorn, and saguaro. Saguaro National Park, Joshua Tree National Park, Cabeza Prieta National Wildlife Refuge, and Kofa National Wildlife Refuge extended the protection.

But the monument bargain brought more than just a few brown-eyed bighorns and stately cacti. It preserved an entire working ecosystem from the depths of Organ Pipe's water table to the tips of its panoramic peaks. Today it fills 516 square miles of irreplaceable space and solitude, of wonder and scenery, and of understanding and beauty. This was first pick. We need only ask: What if Organ Pipe had not been saved...?

But, the monument is not an island or glass-bowled terrarium. It cannot act or live alone. The region affects the monument, just as the monument affects the region. The intricate web of causes and effects is extensive and

Home Again

Desert bighorn ram

incompletely understood. Given its location in the geographical and biological center of the Sonoran Desert, Organ Pipe plays a pivotal role in our larger protection, understanding, and appreciation of this desert.

The monument is at the core of other great reserves and natural areas. In Sonora two neighboring

Hooded oriole

Bobcat

biosphere reserves comprise four million acres covering the Upper Gulf of California, Pinacate, and Gran Desierto. In the United States, the Cabeza Prieta National Wildlife Refuge and the Barry M. Goldwater Air Force Range help protect 2.6 million acres of desert, and the Tohono O'odham Nation is 2.7 million acres. In this tri-cultural region it is not uncommon to have friends who speak three languages: English, Spanish, and O'odham!

An inscription on a tri-national obelisk in Sonoyta reads:

> *In friendship we find purpose.*
> *In honesty we find trust.*
> *In alliance we find strength.*
> *In this desert we find our home.*

Today Organ Pipe remains free and wild, a place saved for the you's and me's of tomorrow. Here we reconfirm what we already knew. The sun is bright. Motion is energizing. Nature remains beautiful. And we're quite alive.

We can walk the trail with the Hohokam, savor shading boughs of sweet acacia, smell the rain on the wind, touch the flare of a flowering ocotillo, and feel the immensity of a deep canyon. We can see twenty shades of green, fairy shrimp in transient pools, the shimmer of illusion across hot ground, velvety red sand mites, and the blur of a prairie falcon on the attack. We can touch the spine of a barrel cactus, hear the thrum of a kangaroo rat's feet, smell the subtle perfumes of night flowers, and taste a raindrop on our tongue.

Organ Pipe is the dessert of deserts. If we've been true, we too qualify as desert rats. Scandinavian explorer Carl Lumholtz knew of other places, having visited the world's busiest cities on four continents. He knew how to hold his fork when dining with royalty, but when he had to leave the Sonoran Desert for home after two years of primitive camping, he kept looking back. He had seen this desert closeup from the seat of a wagon and by the sole of his boots. He had endured its thunderstorms, its bad water, and its heat. From the balcony of the best hotel, he could only shake his head and reflect, "Fond as I am of civilized life and all it implies..., I could not help longing for the fresh, cool, beautiful, and silent nights of my wild desert."

God speed your prompt and safe return. *Buen viaje. 'Ant o a ep 'em-ñei.*

"I walked in the garden often these last days, preferably alone, and looked lovingly at my clumps of brittle-weed, my fine beds of desert holly, my borders of paper daisies and desert marigolds. Here, tended

by unseen hands, grew plants equal to any in a botanical garden. They seemed to flourish for me alone, just as the birds seemed to sing for me alone. There was no one else to see them, just as there was no else to hear the birds sing."

—OLGA WRIGHT SMITH,
Gold on the Desert

Acknowledgements

For Jim: the axle of our wheels. Special thanks to the Organ Pipe staff: Superintendent Harold Smith, Jon Arnold, Matthew Arnold, Jim Barnett, Dominic Cardea, Charles Conner, Mitzi Frank, Kate Garmise, Lesley Moosman, Ami Pate, Aniceto Olais, Tom Potter, Sue Rutman, Doug Sokell, and Tim Tibbitts. Friends of the monument, including Richard Bailowitz, Charles Bowden, Hal Coss, Richard Felger, Floyd Flores, Bill Hartmann, Julian Hayden, Bill Hoy, Peter Kresan, Alex Mintzer, Gary Nabhan, Adrianne Rankin, Joan E. Scott, Sandra Scott, and Caroline Wilson, also helped immensely. This is their book.

Further Reading

These informative and interesting books may be available at your hometown library or at the visitor center bookstore.

Abbey, Edward. 1984. *Beyond the Wall*. New York: Holt, Rinehart, and Winston.

Abbey, Edward. 1973. *Cactus Country*. New York: Time-Life Books.

Annerino, John. 1991. *Adventuring in Arizona*. San Francisco: Sierra Club Books.

Bahr, Donald, Juan Smith, William Smith Allison, and Julian Hayden. 1994. *The Short, Swift Time of Gods on Earth: The Hohokam Chronicles*. Berkeley: University of California Press.

Baylor, Byrd. 1975. *The Desert Is Theirs*. New York: Aladdin Books.

Baylor, Byrd. 1993. *Desert Voices*. New York: Aladdin Books.

Benson, Lyman and Robert A. Darrow. 1981. *Trees and Shrubs of the Southwestern Deserts*. Tucson: University of Arizona Press.

Betancourt, Julio L., Thomas R. Van Devender, and Paul S. Martin. 1990. *Packrat Middens: The Last 40,000 Years of Biotic Change*. Tucson: University of Arizona Press.

Bowden, Charles. 1986. *Blue Desert*. Tucson: University of Arizona Press.

Bowden, Charles. 1985. *Killing the Hidden Waters*. Austin: University of Texas Press.

Bowden, Charles. 1992. *The Sonoran Desert*. New York: Harry Abrams.

Cardea, Dominic. 1995. *Explorers Guide: Organ Pipe Cactus National Monument*. Tucson: Southwest Parks and Monuments Association.

Fontana, Bernard L. 1994. *Entrada: The Legacy of Spain and Mexico in the United States*. Tucson: Southwest Parks and Monuments Association.

Gibson. Arthur C. and Park S. Nobel. 1986. *The Cactus Primer*. Cambridge, Massachusetts: Harvard University Press.

Groschupf, Kathleen D., Bryan T. Brown, and R. Roy Johnson. 1988. *An annotated checklist of the birds of Organ Pipe Cactus National Monument*. Tucson: Southwest Parks and Monuments Association.

Hartmann, William K. 1985. *Desert Heart: Chronicles of the Sonoran Desert*. Tucson: Fisher Books.

Hodge, Carl. 1991. *All about Saguaros*. Phoenix: Arizona Highways.

Hoffmeister, Donald F. 1986. *Mammals of Arizona*. Tucson: University of Arizona Press.

Hornaday, William T. 1983. *Camp-Fires on Desert and Lava*. Tucson: University of Arizona.

Ives, Ronald L. 1989. *Land of Lava, Ash, and Sand*. Tucson: Arizona Historical Society.

Ajo lily

OPPOSITE PAGE: *Brittlebush flowers and saguaro ribs*

Levy, David H. 1994. *The Sky: A User's Guide*. New York: Cambridge University Press.

Lumholtz, Carl. 1990. *New Trails in Mexico*. Tucson: University of Arizona Press.

MacMahon, James A. 1985. *The Audubon Society Nature Guides: Deserts*. New York: Knopf.

Marchand, Peter. 1994. *What Good is a Cactus?* Colorado: Roberts Rinehart.

McGuire, Randall H. and Michael B. Schiffer. 1982. *Hohokam and Patayan: Prehistory of Southwestern Arizona*. New York: Academic Press.

Brewer's blackbirds at Quitobaquito

Nabhan, Gary P., ed. 1993. *Counting Sheep*. Tucson: University of Arizona Press.

Nabhan, Gary P. 1985. *Gathering the Desert*. Tucson: University of Arizona Press.

Nabhan, Gary P. 1982. *The Desert Smells Like Rain*. Tucson: University of Arizona Press.

Nabhan, Gary Paul and John L. Carr. 1994. *Ironwood: An Ecological and Cultural Keystone of the Sonoran Desert*. Washington, D.C.: Conservational International, Occasional Paper No. 1.

Ortiz, Alfonso, ed. 1983. *Handbook of North American Indians: Southwest, vol 10*. Washington, D.C.: Smithsonian Institution.

Polis, Gary A., ed. 1991. *The Ecology of Desert Communities*. Tucson: University of Arizona Press.

Sheridan, Thomas. 1994. *Arizona: A History*. Tucson: University of Arizona Press.

Shreve, Forrest and Ira L. Wiggins. 1964. *Vegetation and Flora of the Sonoran Desert*. Stanford, California: Stanford University Press.

Shubinski, Raymond. 1991. *Discover Arizona's Night Sky*. Phoenix: Arizona Highways Books.

Sutton, Ann and Myron. 1966. *The Life of the Desert*. New York: McGraw-Hill.

Turner, Raymond M., Janice E. Bowers, and Tony L. Burgess. 1995. *Sonoran Desert Plants: An Ecological Atlas*. Tucson: University of Arizona Press.

Van Dyke, John C. 1980. *The Desert*. Salt Lake City, Utah: Peregrine Smith.

Werner, Floyd and Carl Olson. 1994. *Learning About and Living With Insects of the Southwest*. Tucson: Fisher Books.

Wilt, Richard A. 1976. *Birds of Organ Pipe Cactus National Monument*. Globe, Arizona: Southwest Park and Monuments Association.

Woodin, Ann. 1994. *Home is the Desert*. Oracle, Arizona: Oracle Press.

Zwinger, Ann. 1989. *The Mysterious Lands*. New York: Dutton.

Many other books, reports, articles, and papers were indispensable in writing this text, but are not included here because they are technical or not generally available. I am deeply indebted to those researchers and authors.